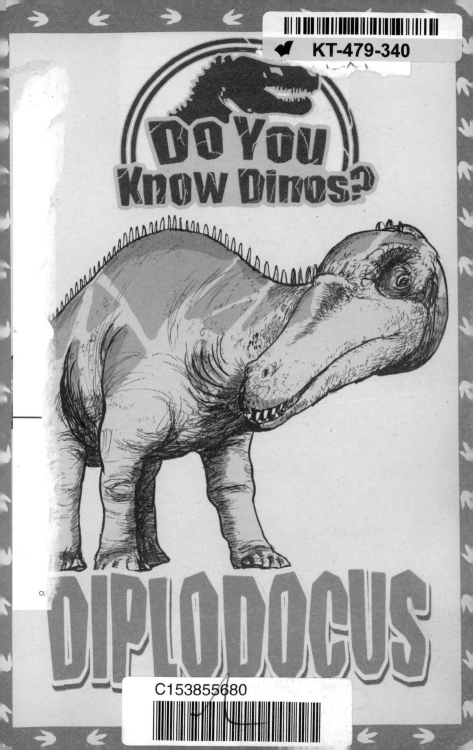

Do You Know Dinos?

DIPLODOCUS

Professor Michael J Benton – dinosaur consultant
Valerie Wilding – educational advisor
Ben Newth – researcher

Scholastic Children's Books,
Euston House, 24 Eversholt Street,
London NW1 1DB, UK

A division of Scholastic Ltd
London ~ New York ~ Toronto ~ Sydney ~ Auckland
Mexico City ~ New Delhi ~ Hong Kong

First published in the UK by Scholastic Ltd, 2003
(as *Now You Know: Diplodocus – the dinosaur with the looong neck*)
This edition published 2010

Text copyright © Helen Greathead, 2003
Illustrations copyright © Mike Spoor, 2003

978 1407 11464 4

All rights reserved
Printed and bound in the UK by CPI Bookmarque, Croydon, Surrey

2 4 6 8 10 9 7 5 3 1

Contents

Introduction

Do you know how to talk dino? It's easier to say dino names in bits:

Di-plod-oh-kus

Say it slowly, then a bit faster. Diplodocus. Now you know the name of a very long dinosaur.

Diplodocus and you

This is part of Diplodocus

This is you

It's difficult to fit you and Diplodocus on the same page. Diplodocus has got a VERY long neck, hasn't it? Some scientists think Diplodocus held its neck straight out in front so its head stayed close to the ground.

Look up and
you can see
another bit of
Diplodocus.
Its body is
nearly ALL
tummy.

Its legs are stubby
and fat.
They have to be
strong to hold up that
huge body.

Hanging over your head is the last bit of Diplodocus – its tail. The tail is even longer than the neck. It is thin and bendy. Diplodocus can swish it from side to side, so you'd better watch out!

Of course, you wouldn't ever meet a real Diplodocus. All dinosaurs died out ages before people lived on Earth.

Diplodocus belonged to a group of dinosaurs called sauropods (sore-oh-pods). They were the biggest creatures EVER to walk on Earth. And the longest!

Diplodocus was taller than a giraffe.
It was much bigger than an elephant.
And a lot longer than a python.

Some scientists think
it could live for up
to 200 years! When a
Diplodocus was born,
it kept on growing. The
older it got, the bigger
it grew. So the oldest
Diplodocus was
absolutely massive.
But why was it so big?

Diplodocus sticks its neck out

There were some good things about being big.

Diplodocus could reach food other creatures couldn't get at.

It could choose its food first.

It didn't have to worry about being attacked.

But there were some bad things about being big, too.

Diplodocus was too heavy to hop, skip, jump or run. It could only walk veeerrry slooowly.

Being heavy meant its bones could crack easily. A cracked bone might mend. But a broken bone meant Diplodocus couldn't move at all. If it didn't move, it couldn't find enough food to feed itself. It would be a dead Diplodocus.

Urk!

Diplodocus had to eat nearly all day to feed its great big body. It had to drink a lot, too. Diplodocus had to keep moving to find food and water. And that's why its long neck was so brilliant...

It could stretch out to reach into a deep, thick forest.

It could reach down into a river to pick out some tasty weeds.

It could gobble up all the leaves and ferns in sight, while the rest of its body stayed put!

But sometimes Diplodocus couldn't
reach the leaves on the taller trees.
So it sat on its back legs and its tail. Then
it lifted its front legs up, and pushed a
whole tree right over!

C-R-E-A-K

Diplodocus looked funny sitting like this. It was too heavy to move fast. But Diplodocus was not as heavy as other sauropods. Its bones were hollow, so they were light, too. That's why, when Diplodocus pushed up on to its back legs, it didn't topple over.

At the end of that very long neck, was a tiny head – with a very small brain. The head of a Diplodocus was not much bigger than your head.

Diplodocus head

Your head

Inside its mouth were some funny, sticky-out teeth. There were only a few of them and they were not very strong. They were long, thin and gappy! But Diplodocus didn't need a dinosaur dentist. Its teeth were like that for a reason.

Diplodocus was a vegetarian dinosaur. It ate almost anything – as long as it was green. When Diplodocus reached up to a tasty looking tree, it opened its mouth and whole branches went in.

Chomp

It clamped its teeth together and pulled back its head. The pine needles, cones and green twigs stayed in its mouth.

Nibble

The tough branches came out again –
through the gaps in the teeth!

Chomp

Diplodocus probably had green bits stuck
between its teeth a lot of the time.

Burp

Diplodocus only had teeth at the front of its mouth. It didn't have any back teeth to chew its food. Instead, it rolled the food around with its tongue and covered it in spit.

Diplodocus needed loads of spit. It probably dribbled most of the time. But the spit was really useful. It held the food together so it could slide easily all the way down into the tummy. Diplodocus didn't want anything to get stuck in its very long neck.

And Diplodocus
swallowed something
else to help its food
go down ...

Splat!

… stones! Lots of them.

The stones helped Diplodocus to chew
… with its tummy! Strong muscles in a
Diplodocus tum churned the food around.
The stones helped to mush up the food.

As the stones whirled round in the huge
Diplodocus tummy, they started to grind
smooth. When they got really smooth
they were no use any more. So Diplodocus
got rid of them in its weird-looking poo.
Then it searched for some new ones,
and started again.

Diplodocus changes the world

Diplodocus travelled as part of a herd. Hundreds of them walked together – very slowly. The herd was very big indeed! And wherever it went, the land it walked on would never be the same again.

Other dinosaurs knew when the herd was coming. They heard a rumbling sound, like thunder. The sound was Diplodocuses breathing, burping and thumping the ground as they walked! It got louder as they moved closer. It was quite scary! But at least other animals had plenty of time to get out of the way. They could hear the herd coming ages before they arrived.

The Diplodocuses ate as they went.
They walked up to forests that looked
like this:

And left them behind looking like this:

What a mess! When Diplodocus left
a forest behind, it wasn't a forest
any more!

But a trampled forest made life easier
for some animals.

Smaller plants grew when the trees
were out of the way. Lots of animals fed
on the smaller plants, and on the tops of
the pushed-over trees.

Meanwhile, Diplodocus kept on moving.
Life for the herd was nearly always the
same. Walk a bit … then eat a bit. Walk
a bit … eat a bit. They didn't have much
reason to stop, except, perhaps, to have …

… a bath!

Sometimes the herd found huge, muddy puddles of water. They knelt down and rolled over in the mud! The bath didn't make them cleaner, but it was great for their skin. It got rid of niggling insects and it kept Diplodocus cool in the hot sun.

But when the huge, heavy dinosaurs climbed out of their bath, the muddy puddle was different...

They had made it deeper and wider, ready to fill up with rain – and turn the muddy puddle into a nice, deep pool!

Diplodocus never forgets

The herd did everything together. The female Diplodocuses even laid their eggs together.

First they found land with some water nearby. This was their nesting ground.

Then they squatted down. They might lay as many as 40 eggs each!

They covered the nest with rotten leaves to keep it warm.

Then they walked off ... leaving behind hundreds and hundreds of eggs.

This was bad news for the Diplodocus eggs. With no adults to guard them, anything could happen! The eggs were only this big:

Diplodocus egg

You

Dipolodocus eggs were great for other dinosaurs to eat. The eggs couldn't run away. And they were full of goodness, too.

Slurp!

So why did the mums leave their babies behind? Well, they had to! A Diplodocus had to keep eating. It had to keep moving to find enough food. If all the mums stayed with their eggs, they would quickly run out of food … and die! And that would not help their babies at all.

So the babies that did hatch out had to find their own food and water. And they were always in danger. The mums laid all those eggs for a good reason. A lot of the eggs got eaten. A lot of the babies got eaten, too. But lots, lots more of them survived.

A newly hatched Diplodocus was not much bigger than a human baby:

Human baby

Diplodocus baby

And next to its mum, baby Dip was ...

… tiny!

Spot the baby

So why couldn't the baby walk with the herd?

A newborn Diplodocus could not walk from one end of its mum to the other, without stopping for a rest.

It might get crushed under mum's enormous feet!

The herd moved slowly, but baby Dip
could never keep up.

As soon as it hatched out, the baby
Diplodocus started eating tasty weeds
from the river and ferns from the bank.
It had to learn to look after itself quickly.
And it needed to eat a lot, because it
was about to start growing like mad.

Baby Dip grew bigger
and bigger and bigger.
And just as it was big
enough to walk
with the
herd ...

... the mums came back! Did they
remember their babies and come back for
them? Or did they just come back to lay
more eggs? Nobody knows for sure. But
this time, when the herd moved on, the
little ones went, too.

47

Diplodocus dies

Even with the herd, a young Diplodocus was not out of danger.

Allosaurus was a meat-eating dinosaur. It had long, sharp teeth. It had deadly claws. And Allosaurus liked the taste of Diplodocus meat.

An Allosaurus might follow the herd, hoping to find a dead Diplodocus.

But if a Diplodocus didn't die by itself, Allosaurus might have to attack it. So Allosaurus hid … and waited. It waited for a young Diplodocus … or a sick Diplodocus, or a very, very old Diplodocus, to trail behind the herd.

A weak Diplodocus could still fight. It could sit back on its legs and tail, and thump down on Allosaurus with its front legs.

Thump

It could jab Allosaurus with the spike on each of its front feet.

Bash

It could use its tail a bit like a whip ...
to slash through Allosaurus's skin!

Mmm
Thwack

But a weak Diplodocus got tired
quickly. It was easier for
Allosaurus to kill. And it
was worth the effort.
One Diplodocus
would keep
Allosaurus well
fed for days.

Allosaurus was a danger to Diplodocus. But something else was far more deadly …

It wasn't another dinosaur. It wasn't even an animal. Diplodocus was in most danger from … the weather!

When Diplodocus lived, there were only two seasons – wet and dry.

If the rains started in the north, Diplodocus travelled south. When the rains came in the south, Diplodocus travelled north again.

But sometimes the rains didn't come at all. Without water, the leaves and ferns started to wither and die. The lakes and rivers dried up.

There was nothing to eat or drink. The herd was huge. It took a lot of food to feed all those dinosaurs. When the food died, the dinosaurs died, too – by the hundred. The weather could kill the whole herd.

Diplodocus starts some arguments

Life was tough for Diplodocus. But Diplodocus was a survivor. We know, because there are loads of Diplodocus fossils to prove it. The fossils show that there were once thousands and thousands of Diplodocuses!

Fossils are bones or traces of dinosaurs, like a footprint, or a tail trail, that have turned to rock over millions of years.

Samuel
Williston

A dinosaur hunter called Samuel Williston found the first Diplodocus fossils in 1877, in North America. It was named Diplodocus by dinosaur expert, O.C. Marsh. The name means "double beamed".

O.C. Marsh

The name comes from the strange shape of the bones underneath Diplodocus's tail. The bones looked like this:

Scientists once thought the bones protected the tail as it trailed along the ground. But now they're not sure what they were for ... because they know Diplodocus didn't drag its tail at all!

And that's just one Diplodocus fact that scientists have argued about.

In 1899, a millionaire called Andrew Carnegie paid for the fossilized bones of a whole Diplodocus to be put back together again. He displayed the skeleton in his own museum. It was ENORMOUS! Everybody wanted to see it.

Carnegie had a great idea. He sent models of Diplodocus to museums around the world.

But the models were finished in a hurry. And the skeleton had some bones missing. The Diplodocus models ended up with the wrong front feet! They were the back feet of a dinosaur called Camarasaurus!

right foot

wrong foot

Scientists wanted to find out more about Diplodocus. But they often got the facts wrong. Some thought Diplodocus was too heavy to walk on land. They said it lived in deep lakes, and that only its eyes and its nostrils poked out of the water – so it could breathe and see!

Other scientists thought this was nonsense! And when fossilized footprints of Diplodocus were found, they finally proved that:

Diplodocus walked on land.

Diplodocus lived with a herd.

Diplodocus didn't drag its tail.

Until just a few years ago, Diplodocus was always shown with its nostrils on the top of its head. Like this:

Nostrils

But a scientist, called Lawrence Witmer, did a study of dinosaur noses! He discovered that Diplodocus's nostrils were not on the top of its head, after all. They were just where you'd expect to find them. On the front of its face.

Nostrils

Most scientists now agree that Witmer was right. But there are still lots of things they don't agree on. And the one creature that knows all the answers swished its long tail for the last time millions and millions of years ago.

DINONEWS

DETAILS DAY–TO–DAY DINO DISCOVERIES.

ALL NEW DINO FINDS!

Scientific theories – a pain in the neck?

Dipolodocus diet

Sauropod discovered!

STOP PRESS!
SCIENTISTS' THEORIES A PAIN IN THE NECK

Over 100 years ago scientists said: Diplodocus stood with its neck sticking up.

About twelve years ago they said: Diplodocus stood with its neck out straight.

NOW they're back to saying: Diplodocus stood with its neck sticking up... Why can't they make up their minds?

A research team from the University of Portsmouth argues that there was no point having a great long neck if you couldn't hold it up to:

- see for miles
- look for food and spot danger coming
- nibble at the leaves on very tall trees

But they agree Diplodocus could stick its neck out straight to get a drink of water. They say their study of birds and mammals that are alive today proves their point.

Other scientists still insist that there's no way this giant dino could lift up its head. It would make pumping blood to the brain too difficult. They say, if Diplodocus lifted its head up high, it would probably die!

NEW SAUROPOD DISCOVERED ... ON MUSEUM SHELF

You don't need to go digging in a quarry, or scouring the seashore, to make an amazing dino discovery. University student Mike Taylor was looking behind the displays at London's Natural History Museum when he noticed something unusual.

It was a fossil. Definitely part of the backbone of a sauropod, but definitely not one he'd come across before. In fact, it was a new type of sauropod altogether. And it had been sitting on a museum shelf for over 100 years!

DIPLODOCUS ON A DIET

We already know that Diplodocus was much lighter than other dinos in its sauropod family. Brachiosaurus and Apatosaurus were slightly smaller but much, much heavier than Diplodocus.

Now, Gary Packard, from Colorado State University, says most dinos were slimmer than we thought. Only the hard parts of the body, like bones and teeth turn to fossils over time. Scientists use those fossils to work out how big a dinosaur really was when all its flesh was in place. This means doing some complicated sums. And Gary Packard reckons they've been getting those sums wrong!

Using Gary's calculations, Apatosaurus was less than half as heavy as scientists first thought, and lightweight Diplodocus was one and a half tonnes slimmer!

THE BIGGEST DINOSAUR EVER

We know that the sauropod family was the biggest family of dinosaurs EVER. But was Diplodocus the biggest dinosaur? The answer is nope. Probably not.

Diplodocus was very, very long. It might have had the longest tail – made up of over 80 bones! But some bigger dinos have been found:

- One called Supersaurus had a much longer neck than Diplodocus and a shoulder blade that was bigger than the man who found it.
- One called Sauroposeidon (sore-oh-pos-eye-don) is probably the tallest dinosaur ever found.
- One called Argentinosaurus is thought to be the biggest dinosaur ever discovered.

But, wait a minute, in 2006 there was yet another discovery… Trouble is, we only have a few bones to show for each of these gigantic dinos so we can't be certain of their size. And at any time a dino dig might turn up a creature that's bigger still. So let's give Diplodocus first prize for being:

THE LONGEST DINO THAT'S BEEN DISCOVERED WITH A COMPLETE SKELETON – SO FAR…

Di-yes/Di-no quiz

You've read the book, so these puzzles will be eea-sy! Just answer "di-yes" or "di-no" to each of these sentences:

1 Diplodocus could slash its tail like a whip at any attackers. Di-yes/Di-no
2 Diplodocus dribbled nearly all the time. Di-yes/Di-no
3 Diplodocus was a caring parent who looked after its babies for their first two years. Di-yes/Di-no
4 Diplodocus was the biggest creature that ever walked the earth. Di-yes/Di-no
5 Diplodocus eggs were huge. Bigger than a spacehopper. Di-yes/Di-no
6 Diplodocus liked to keep itself spotlessly clean at all times. Di-yes/Di-no

7 Diplodocus ate leaves, ferns, pine cones and … stones. Di-yes/Di-no

8 Diplodocus had nostrils on its forehead. Di-yes/Di-no

9 Allosaurus was smaller than Diplodocus, but it still liked to attack and eat the giant dino. Di-yes/Di-no

10 If Diplodocus didn't keep moving it would die! Di-yes/Di-no

Answers

1 Di-yes it could! (See page 51)

2 Di-yes it did! (See page 24)

3 Di-no it definitely wasn't! (See pages 36–39)

4 Di-no actually, it wasn't. (See page 71)

5 Di-no they weren't. (See page 39)

6 Oh, di-no it didn't! (See pages 34–35)

7 Oh di-yes it did. (See pages 25–26)

8 Di-no it didn't. (See page 63)

9 Di-yes it did! (See page 51)

10 Di-yes it would! (See page 40)

Spot the Dino Difference

Look at these two pictures carefully. Can you find ten differences?

ANSWERS

Spot the Difference

How many did you spot?

Diplodosearch

```
S E L B B I R D O P R N D
L O N G T A I L S A G T I
I P Z O F S E B G L S K P
R W H A J E C D I U R V L
T R T E S N L M R J I Q O
S L A X T O M U A R E B D
O C B J I T A G F U M L O
N L D W Z S L A F U B R C
S A U R O P O D E X A P U
R N M T S V E S C D W I S
J L A M T R U D F E R L Y
I P S N O M T A J I N E D
A L L O S A U R U S O P H
```

ALLOSAURUS	**LONG TAIL**
APATOSAURUS	MUDBATH
DIPLODOCUS	**MUSEUM**
DRIBBLE	NOSTRILS
GIRAFFE	**SAUROPOD**
HERD	STONES

There are twelve words, or pairs of words, hidden in this Diplodosearch. Look at the list above and see if you can find them all. It's not easy! They might be written up, down, backwards, forwards or diagonally.

ANSWERS

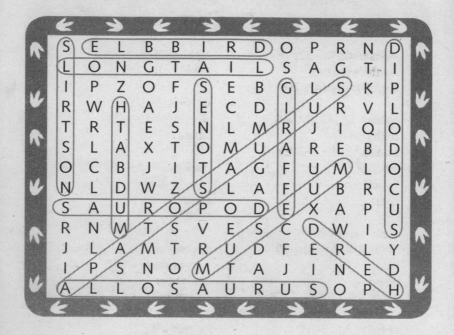

```
S E L B B I R D O P R N D
L O N G T A I L S A G T I
 I P Z O F S E B G L S K P
 I R W H A J E C D I U R V L
R T A E S T L M R J I Q O
S L A X T N M U A R E B D
O N C B J I T A F U M L O
N L D W Z S L A F B R C
S A U R O P O D E X A P U
R N M T S V E S C D W I S
J L A M T R U D F E R L Y
I S N O M T A J I N E D
A L L O S A U R U S O P H
```

Do You Know Dinos?

Index

"These books ... provide a great deal of information in a highly accessible way using a small amount of easily read text imaginatively combined with plenty of line drawings ... a good choice for dinosaur fans who are also reluctant readers as well as those who are already enthusiastic." *Wordpool News*